YOU DON'T NEED BANGS YOU NEED A Life Coach

Embrace Your Journey, Overcome
Obstacles & Create a Life You Love

JODY O'DELL

Synergy Publishing Group
Belmont, North Carolina

Contents

Introduction:
Hey, Beautiful Soul!

It's an absolute joy to connect with you. I'm Jody, and I've walked through life's twists and turns armed with a spirit of resilience, a dash of rebellion, and an unshakable belief that life is meant to be extraordinary. This journal is a celebration of our shared journey—a journey that often requires courage, grit, and the guiding light of a life coach to help us uncover our full potential.

In this guided journal, you'll find seven core lessons. These lessons are derived from my stories and journey as a hair dresser turned life coach. They have become foundational to the ways that I have supported myself and others! You'll see the following in each lesson:

1. An initial journal prompt to get you thinking and reflecting about an element of your life.
2. A story from my life that connects to the theme of each lesson.
3. An action step following each lesson's story to get you to draw, write, and explore using the very same coaching tools I use with my clients.

I encourage you to find your best time of day to work through each lesson. Take your time. Leave space for yourself to be with yourself.

Ready? Let's dive in!

With love,

Jody

Lesson 1:
Nurture Your Dreams

5-Minute Journal Prompt

**If there were no rules, limitations, or judgments,
what dreams would you pursue?**

Set a timer. Write fast. See what shows up. ZERO judgment here.

....

....

....

....

....

....

....

....

....

....

....

....

....

....

....

....

....

....

....

....

....

....

....

....

....

....

....

....

....

....

....

....

....

....

....

....

....

....

Born to Explore:
The Mountain Girl with a
Heart Full of Dreams

In the heart of the Western North Carolina mountains lies the quaint town of Brevard, a place that would shape my perspective on life in ways I never could have imagined. From the beginning, I was raised with a unique philosophy that championed the importance of trying new things, taking risks, and thinking outside of the box. This philosophy would become the cornerstone of my journey, propelling me toward a life rich with experiences and a mindset open to endless possibilities.

My childhood was a symphony of freedom and exploration. With its lush forests, winding trails, and clear blue skies, Brevard was a playground that beckoned me to venture into the unknown. Even before mountain biking became a global phenomenon, I pedaled through these trails, forging a connection with nature that would fuel my passion for adventure. Camping under star-studded skies, fishing in tranquil mountain streams, and riding dirt bikes along thrilling, winding trails—these were not mere activities, but rather profound lessons in embracing the curiosity of the unfamiliar.

As I look back on those formative years, it's clear that my parents played a pivotal role in shaping my outlook. Their unwavering support and encouragement formed the bedrock upon which my adventurous spirit was built. It wasn't just that they allowed me to explore; they actively participated, instilling in me the belief that curiosity was a gift to be nurtured, not suppressed. Their actions taught me that it was okay to step off the well-trodden path and carve out my own journey, even if it led to uncharted territories.

Summers were a time of vacations, encompassing long car rides ending at beautiful destinations. Some trips included seaside escapades, a complete departure from the mountain haven that was Brevard. These coastal retreats introduced me to the allure of the beach, the rhythmic crashing of waves, and the boundless expanse of the ocean. The contrast between the mountains and the coast showcased the beauty of diversity, not just in landscapes but in experiences. During these getaways, I fell in love with the idea of living without boundaries. This mindset would prove invaluable as I navigated the challenges and opportunities ahead.

Through it all, my family remained my constant, unwavering support system. Their belief in me transcended all else, giving me the confidence to chase dreams that seemed audacious to others. Their applause was my motivation, their presence my strength. It wasn't just about cheering from the sidelines; they actively participated in my journey, guiding me when I stumbled and celebrating my victories with unbridled joy.

As the years went by and I ventured into new terrain—figuratively and literally—the lessons I imbibed in those early days remained my compass. The ability to embrace the unknown, take risks with a hopeful heart, and approach challenges with an open mind became my signature. Every mountain I climbed, every wave I rode, and every endeavor I undertook echoed the wisdom I had gathered from my childhood in Brevard.

As I reflect now on the crossroads of my past and present, I realize that the spirit of adventure cultivated in those North Carolina mountains still burns brightly within me. The lessons of embracing the unconventional path, chasing dreams that others might deem impossible, and wholeheartedly believing in the power of exploring new horizons have become the touchstones of my journey. As I look forward to the road ahead, I do so with the same eager anticipation that propelled me to pedal down those trails, cast my fishing line into the unknown, and build forts in the woods.

In a world that often encourages conformity, my upbringing in Brevard taught me that the outliers, the dreamers, and the risk-takers create the most vibrant stories. The path less traveled is not just a metaphor; it's a roadmap to a life lived authentically, passionately, and without regrets. And for that, I owe a debt of gratitude to the mountains, the coast, and most importantly, the family who nurtured my belief in the extraordinary potential of an adventurous life.

5-Minute Reflective Prompt

Now, take a moment to draw your authentic, passionate, risk-taking roadmap. Sit with your map for a bit, and then make a list of feelings that show up around it.

Lesson 2:
Nurturing Roots of Resilience and Love

5-Minute Journal Prompt

Write about your roots—all of them—the good and the not-so-good!

Set a timer. Write fast. See what shows up. ZERO judgment here.

....

....

....

....

....

....

....

....

....

....

....

....

....

....

....

....

....

....

Lessons from a Legacy of Love

As the eldest of three siblings, my early life was framed by the culture in our small Southern town and the delicate balance of my parents' dual roles. Dad, a dedicated employee at the paper mill, shouldered the responsibilities of his day job and a small family business. Mom, with her managerial role at a group home for developmentally disabled adults, brought compassion and care to those who needed it most, all while helping manage our family's business endeavors. This blend of diligence and empathy taught me some of life's most important lessons.

My parents taught us that work was more than just clocking in and out. It demonstrated character, an embodiment of values, and a pursuit that deserved utmost dedication. Their work ethic was unwavering, a testament to their commitment to providing us with a secure and nurturing environment. But amid the responsibilities and commitments, they emphasized that work must always be harmonized with family time and moments of shared joy.

Their desire to offer us a brighter future was palpable. They often spoke about their upbringing, challenges, and determination to break those cycles. My parents understood that their roles extended far beyond breadwinning; they were architects of dreams, shaping a landscape of possibilities for my siblings and I to explore. Their sacrifices were an investment in our potential, a testament to their belief that we could reach for the stars with hard work, empathy, and love.

In this landscape of guidance and wisdom, my grandmother emerged as a beacon of strength as well. Her memory still casts a profound influence on my life. She was a woman who had weathered the storm of escaping a physically abusive marriage and raising a daughter, my mother, entirely on her own. She emerged not broken but transformed. Her life story embodied resilience, a tale of refusing to be defined by her hardships.

Through her example, I learned that life's challenges need not mold us into vessels of bitterness and anger. Instead, they can be catalysts for the creation of something beautiful. My grandmother chose to cultivate a legacy of love and kindness, transforming her pain into a force for good. Her legacy echoed that of a quiet revolution, proving that strength lies not in vengeance but in rising above and creating a new narrative.

It was from her that I gleaned a lesson in grace, in the enduring power of forgiveness. Her life was a testament to the profound impact a single individual can have on those around them. Through her actions, she showed me that life's difficulties need not be the final chapter of our story; we hold the pen, and we can choose to rewrite our narratives with love and compassion.

As I journey through life, I carry the lessons of my parents and my grandmother with me. Their examples form the foundation of my values and aspirations. From my parents, I inherited the fusion of hard work and empathy, the understanding that success is measured in achievements and the lives we touch. From my grandmother, I learned that even in the face of adversity, we possess the strength to rise, heal, and share love unconditionally.

This chapter of my life story is a tribute to those who came before me and carved the path I walk today. It's a testament to the power of role models and their profound impact on our characters and the world around us. Reflecting on their legacies, I am reminded that our stories are interconnected and woven through time and experience. And through it all, the threads of love, resilience, and the pursuit of a better tomorrow continue to bind us together.

5-Minute Reflective Prompt

Draw a family tree with your roots, foundations, and values. Sit with that drawing a bit. List what in your past helps you navigate your future.

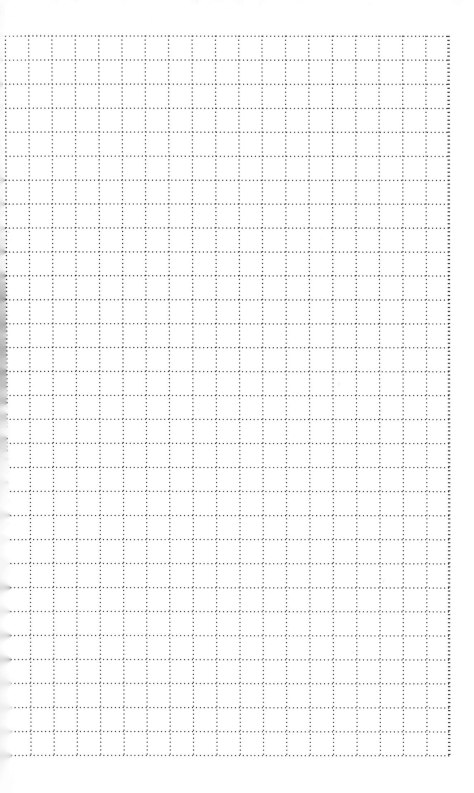

Lesson 3:
Coloring Outside the Lines

5-Minute Journal Prompt

Have you ever allowed yourself to color outside the lines? Yes? What did that look like? No? Why not?

Set a timer. Write fast. See what shows up. ZERO judgment here.

....

....

....

....

....

....

....

....

....

....

....

....

....

....

....

....

....

Embracing the Unexpected Journey

Life has a way of surprising us when we least expect it. After the rigors of high school, I found myself standing at the threshold of adulthood, facing the question that has perplexed countless young minds: "What's next?" While some of my peers were diving headfirst into college degrees and traditional career paths, I felt a magnetic pull toward a different kind of canvas—one where creativity, style, and personal expression intersected. And so my journey led me to the Avant-Garde College of Cosmetology in the sun-kissed realm of Myrtle Beach, South Carolina.

Nestled against the backdrop of rolling waves and endless stretches of sand, Avant-Garde College of Cosmetology beckoned like a promise of transformation. As I embarked on this new chapter of my life, I was met with many experiences that would shape my future in ways I could scarcely imagine.

In 1991, with a diploma and dreams of breathing life into hair as an art form, I entered the bustling world of beauty and style. My first post-graduation gig was at a local salon and spa in Myrtle Beach, where I honed my craft and learned to see hair not merely as strands to be manipulated but as a medium through which individuals could express their unique identities.

But life is never content with just one chapter, and as the year unfolded, I entered another transformative phase. The same year I received my cosmetology degree, I also exchanged vows with my high school sweetheart. The path of love and partnership was now intertwined with my professional journey as we faced the thrilling yet challenging prospect of building a life together.

Just six months after our wedding, the tides of destiny swept us away to Charlotte, North Carolina. This city would become the canvas upon which my skills would truly blossom. In Charlotte,

I joined the Carmen Carmen Salon, a prestigious establishment renowned for its commitment to innovation and artistry. Here, I would discover my true potential as a hairstylist.

Under the guidance of experienced mentors, and alongside a team of like-minded artists, I immersed myself in the techniques of Vidal Sassoon and Toni & Guy. These methods weren't just about cutting and styling; they were about elevating hairdressing to an art form. My passion for my work was further fueled by my role on the Artistic Team, where I had the privilege of training new stylists, contributing to photo shoots that brought visions to life, and stepping onto the stage at hair shows to showcase my craft.

As if that weren't enough, I discovered even more unexpected avenues for my passion. From crafting hairdos for local television appearances to working behind the scenes on video shoots, every moment allowed me to expand my horizons and embrace the limitless possibilities my chosen path had to offer. My dreams of traveling, demonstrating, and teaching for a renowned hair company were within arms reach.

But life, ever the master of twists and turns, had different plans for me. As I set my sights on a new trajectory, the Universe presented me with a crossroads. A personal event unfolded, demanding my attention and redefining my priorities: I became pregnant! As the currents of change swept through my life again, I realized that sometimes, the most profound growth occurs when we surrender to the unexpected.

So my journey took an unexpected turn—one that would teach me that the twists and turns of life are not detours, but rather integral parts of the adventure. As I navigated this season of change, I learned to lean into the uncertainty, drawing strength from the resilience I had honed throughout my journey.

My time at Avant-Garde College of Cosmetology, my experiences in the salons of Myrtle Beach and Charlotte, and even the unexpected pregnancy that temporarily shifted my trajectory all wove together to form the tapestry of my story. The journey was far from over, and as I understand it, the path to becoming isn't linear—it's a canvas painted with strokes of discovery, challenges, and the beauty of the unknown.

5-Minute Reflective Prompt

Paint or draw a representation of your life's journey so far. Detail the strokes of beauty, discovery, and challenges. Let it be messy; you don't have to be an artist! Sit with this painting for a bit. List your thoughts, feelings, and reflections on the canvas of your life

Lesson 4:
Challenges
Are Opportunities

5-Minute Journal Prompt

Make a quick list: what unforeseen events have popped up in your life?

Set a timer. Write fast. See what shows up. ZERO judgment here.

....

....

....

....

....

....

....

....

....

....

....

....

....

....

....

....

....

The Power of Reinvention

Life has a peculiar way of weaving unexpected threads into the tapestry of our existence, altering the course we believed we were charting. When I welcomed my daughter, Devin, into the world just three weeks before my twenty-third birthday, I couldn't have foreseen the extraordinary journey.

Motherhood had never been a dream of mine, and the challenges that Devin's arrival brought were not part of the script I had written. Then, when she was six months old, I received the news that would forever change the trajectory of our lives: Devin had special needs. My heart ached for her, yet amid the initial shock, a new chapter of strength and resilience began to unfold.

It wasn't until fifteen years later that she received the official diagnosis of Cohen Syndrome, a rare genetic disorder characterized by developmental delays, intellectual disabilities, and a distinct set of physical features. Those early years were marked by uncertainty, countless doctor's appointments, therapy sessions, and a labyrinth of medical terminology. The world I thought I understood transformed into a landscape of medical codes and therapeutic interventions. Through it all, Devin's courage and the unconditional love we shared propelled me forward.

As I navigated the maze of Devin's needs, my journey of personal growth mirrored hers. Becoming a mother at a young age thrust me into adulthood with unparalleled speed. While my peers were navigating the waters of early adulthood, I balanced formula bottles and therapy appointments. The naive aspirations of my youth collided with the gravity of my responsibilities, urging me to mature in ways I could never have imagined.

Amidst the trials, I began to view the world through a different lens. Life's ordinary triumphs and hardships took on a new meaning. Watching Devin fight battles with her body daily, I realized the preciousness of health and the fragility of human existence. The small moments became significant treasures: the sound of Devin's laughter, her unwavering determination, and the warmth of her embrace. These became the markers of a life beautifully lived, regardless of the challenges we faced.

In 1996, a decision presented itself that would further alter my path. Leaving behind Carmen Carmen, a dream I had poured my heart into, I took the daunting leap to start The Venue, a salon of my own. The need to be in charge of my time to accommodate Devin's increasing medical demands led me to make a choice that I initially saw as surrendering my ambitions for her well-being. Little did I know that this sacrifice would open doors to unforeseen opportunities.

The journey of self-discovery also led me to embrace my role as an educator for the companies Wella and Keune. Sharing my passion for hairstyling and coloring with others became a source of fulfillment and empowerment. The chair that held my clients also held their stories, and in those moments, we built connections that transcended the strands of hair we touched. As I honed my skills as a master colorist, I discovered that life, like hair, could be transformed into something vibrant and beautiful, even when faced with unexpected twists and turns.

Through the ebb and flow of life, my salon and its clients remained my steadfast companions. When the weight of Devin's diagnosis and the challenges that came with it threatened to overwhelm me, the sanctuary of The Venue provided solace and stability. As I sculpted hair, I also sculpted a sanctuary of resilience, where stories were shared, burdens lightened, and dreams reshaped.

I often reflect on how my business and I grew up together. In my mid-twenties, I dove into the sea of entrepreneurship without a clue about balancing a checkbook. Yet, through the years, as I nurtured my business, it in turn nurtured me. The salon became a haven and much more than a business: it was where I found myself. And remarkably, that journey led me to a place I once only dreamt of—a beach house. In 2017, I was able to purchase a beach house. It stands as a testament to my endless hours of work not only at the salon but also on myself. It encompasses my trials and triumphs, the tears and laughter that constitute the pages of my life story.

Ultimately, the story of Devin, The Venue, and me is one of transformation, adaptation, and unexpected growth. Life demanded that we rise to challenges we never thought we were equipped to face, and in doing so, we found the strength to rewrite our narrative. Devin's unique journey illuminated the beauty of life's unpredictable cadence, teaching me that love and determination can create miracles out of seemingly impossible circumstances.

5-Minute Reflective Prompt

Draw a navigational chart of your transformations, adaptations, and unexpected growth. Imagine you are about to set sail. Sit with your chart. Make a quick list of how the course you've created feels.

Lesson 5:
Rebuilding in the Shadow of Loss

5-Minute Journal Prompt

Draw two large hearts side by side. In the one on the left, write the names of loved ones you've lost. In the one on the right, write the things you love about yourself. Sit with this drawing for a bit and write about what you notice.

Set a timer. Write fast. See what shows up. ZERO judgment here.

....

....

....

....

....

....

....

....

....

....

....

....

....

....

....

Weathering the Storms

Life has a peculiar way of thrusting us into periods of profound darkness, where the weight of grief and challenges can feel insurmountable. The years 2009 and 2010 stand as a testament for me that even in despair, the human spirit can find the strength to rebuild, redefine, and emerge stronger than before.

For me, those two years were a crucible of heartache and upheaval. In June 2009, I faced the unthinkable: the loss of my mother to the cruel clutches of cancer. She had been my anchor, confidante, and source of unwavering support. In times of need, her presence had always been a comforting embrace. As the void of her absence engulfed me, I found myself grappling not only with the sorrow of her passing, but also with the realization that I was now navigating life's challenges without her steady hand to guide me.

As the world continued to turn, the following year dealt me another staggering blow. In May 2010, I made the agonizing decision to separate from my husband of nineteen years. The man I had once shared dreams and laughter with had become ensnared in the clutches of alcoholism, his behavior turning increasingly abusive. The dissolution of our marriage was not just the end of a partnership, but also the dismantling of a life I had known for decades. The man who had been my best friend since I was sixteen was no longer recognizable in the person standing before me.

With each passing day, the challenges mounted, and I was left alone in Charlotte's sprawling city. The landscape of my life had shifted, leaving me with a house that once felt like a home, a business that required my dedication, a golden retriever whose loyalty remained unwavering, and a daughter who needed her mother more than ever. It was a daunting array of responsibilities, but the weight of these challenges only ignited a newfound resolve within me.

Armed with a determination to overcome, I embarked on a journey of self-reliance and resilience. The year 2011 brought with it a turning point. As I turned forty, I marked not just the passage of time but also the emergence of a stronger, more self-assured version of myself. The divorce was finalized, bringing closure to a chapter that had left scars both visible and hidden. And then, as if guided by a cosmic force, I crossed paths with a man who would change the trajectory of my life in the most unexpected ways.

The years 2009 and 2010 may have sucked the life out of me, but they also set the stage for a renaissance of the self—one that would teach me the true meaning of resilience and the extraordinary capacity of the human heart.

5-Minute Reflective Prompt

Share how you've rebuilt your life after facing a loss.

Lesson 6:
Finding Love Again

5-Minute Journal Prompt

In what ways have you opened your heart to new possibilities? What was that journey like?

Set a timer. Write fast. See what shows up. ZERO judgment here.

....

....

....

....

....

....

....

....

....

....

....

....

....

....

....

....

When Things Aren't as Easy as They Seem

Chris, who would later become my husband, entered my life with a complex history of challenges and hardships. He was in the midst of a divorce when we first crossed paths, and he had a young daughter. Our instant and intense connection led to him move in with me just three months after our initial date. During our four months of cohabitation, I discovered that his divorce was a result of his wife's infidelity, which had driven him to excessive drinking. Although it wasn't immediately apparent, it became clear over time that Chris, like my ex-husband, was struggling with alcoholism. However, his case was unique, marked by extreme highs and lows.

To protect myself from another relationship with an alcoholic, I established boundaries, and we eventually parted ways. Over the following eight years, we experienced extended periods of no contact, only to reunite later. I glimpsed an incredible man hidden behind Chris's turbulent life, and he repeatedly attempted to regain control of his life, only to see it unravel once more. It was evident that there was more to his struggles than just alcoholism, but the doctors he consulted focused on treating his depression and not his manic episodes.

Meanwhile, I reached a breaking point, realizing that my involvement with him was eroding my self-esteem. I had no choice but to sever all ties. We didn't speak for a year until we coincidentally ran into each other, rekindling an immediate spark. Just one month after that chance encounter, the pandemic hit the world. My daughter, Devin, and I sought refuge at the beach where Chris was residing. He offered to assist with grocery shopping, sparing me from taking Devin to stores, which I accepted reluctantly due to his lack of progress in his personal issues.

During those two months at the beach, Chris and I mended our friendship, and he confessed that he was finally ready for a better life. Fortunately, free mental health services were available via Zoom because of the pandemic, and Chris seized the opportunity. I supported him by researching phone numbers and cheering him on as he reclaimed his life step-by-step. Chris connected with wonderful people eager to help him and followed their guidance. In May 2020, he entered a five-day detox program, where he not only achieved sobriety but also started medication to address his officially diagnosed mental illness. Identifying the root cause of Chris's behavior and treating it allowed him to reclaim his life.

Today, Chris is unashamed to acknowledge his bipolar disorder and alcoholism because he found answers and reclaimed his life. He has transformed into an exceptionally stable, happy, and optimistic individual who cherishes every day. Our paths converged at a point where healing was paramount, and we discovered comfort in each other's presence. We understood the depths of suffering life could impose, and together, we embarked on a healing journey that was both cathartic and transformative.

However, our path to marriage was far from swift. The scars of our past ran deep, requiring time to heal. Therapy became our guiding light, leading us through a maze of emotions, assisting us in confronting the ghosts of our histories, and ultimately bringing us to a place of acceptance and growth.

Eleven years after our initial meeting, we stood before one another, hands joined in a commitment that symbolized the union of two lives and the culmination of years of struggle and triumph. Our love story wasn't a fairy tale but one of resilience, redemption, and the unwavering strength of the human spirit.

Reflecting on those tumultuous years, it's evident that our trials weren't meant to break us but to shape us into individuals capable of rising from the ashes. Loss and heartache may have marked the beginning of that chapter, but our determination, our willingness to confront our demons, and the healing power of love defined its conclusion.

5-Minute Reflective Prompt

Draw a bed of smoldering coals. In the smoke, write all the
ways you've worked on yourself. Sit with your drawing
for a bit. Take a moment and celebrate the work you've
done. Write a few words about how this makes you feel.

Lesson 7:
Live Unapologetically

5-Minute Journal Prompt

What makes you who you are? Make a list of all the gifts you have to share with the world.

Set a timer. Write fast. See what shows up. ZERO judgment here.

....

....

....

....

....

....

....

....

....

....

....

....

....

....

....

....

Weaving Beauty and Purpose

Turning 50 was a turning point. As I embraced my age and wisdom, I realized life was too short to conform to anyone else's expectations. I married the man of my dreams and decided to share my journey with the world, not just through my salon, but also as a life coach.

Life is a journey that takes us down various paths through twists and turns I never reasonably expected. As I sit here, splitting my time between the vibrant city of Charlotte and the serene shores of Carolina Beach, I can't help but marvel at how far this journey has taken me. From a young stylist with a passion for hair to a seasoned professional juggling two successful salon careers and an online coaching business, my story is one of evolution, determination, and a commitment to transforming lives.

In the early days of my career, I was consumed by the artistry of hairstyling. The salon was my canvas, and each client's hair was a unique masterpiece waiting to be created. The satisfaction of helping someone look and feel their best was immeasurable. But as the years rolled by, I began to sense a more profound yearning within me—a calling to utilize life's lessons to make a broader impact.

It was in 2004 that a chance conversation with my dear friend Barb led me to discover the teachings of Tony Robbins. Little did I know that this encounter would catalyze my transformational journey. Robbins' insights ignited a fire within me to seek more than just superficial beauty; I wanted to tap into the wellspring of human potential and guide others to do the same. Attending his Unleash the Power Within seminar in 2005 was a turning point. Walking on fire was a symbolic act of conquering fear and realizing the power of the mind. The experience was exhilarating, but the actual shift happened within me.

Over the years, I became a seeker, actively pursuing personal development and growth. Life coaches entered my life, each serving as a guiding light during different phases. Through their guidance, I learned to navigate challenges, overcome limiting beliefs, and tap into reservoirs of strength I never knew existed. These mentors showed me the profound impact coaching could have on one's journey. I felt compelled to share this revelation with others to help them find their paths toward fulfillment and success.

In 2021, I returned to Unleash the Power Within, not as a novice but as someone with a decade of experience, insights, and a renewed passion for transformation. My journey came full circle; this time, I broke a board in half with my bare hand, symbolizing my commitment to the path of growth and change. Yet, this time, it was accompanied by a deep desire to give back, to pay forward the wisdom I had gained.

This burning desire led me to pursue a BodyMind Coaching certification. Armed with the tools to facilitate holistic transformation, I embarked on a new career chapter. Through my online coaching business, I began to help others bridge the gap between inner and outer beauty. I learned that true transformation occurs when we align our thoughts, emotions, and actions, paving the way for a life filled with purpose, joy, and fulfillment.

As I split my time between the bustling energy of Charlotte and the calming embrace of Carolina Beach, I find myself living my purpose each day. My clients don't just leave with stunning hair; they leave with renewed confidence and a belief in their ability to shape their destiny. My online coaching clients don't just gain insight; they experience profound shifts that empower them to break free from self-imposed limitations.

My journey is a testament to the power of embracing change, the value of seeking wisdom, and the profound impact one can have by living a life of purpose. It's a reminder that our experiences can be woven together to create a tapestry of transformation, no matter how diverse. The path might be winding, but it's the twists and turns that shape us into who we are meant to be.

So, as I stand at this crossroads between hairstyling and coaching, city lights and ocean waves, I am reminded of the words that have guided me on this remarkable journey: "Live a life you love!" With every client I touch and every coaching session I facilitate, I am reminded that beauty isn't just in the hair or the appearance, but in the transformation of lives that radiate with purpose, authenticity, and the pursuit of a life well-lived.

5-Minute Reflective Prompt

Create a collage of all the things that make you amazing.
You can include pictures or words to describe yourself,
the person your life's events have created. Think
of it like a vision board of affirmation for yourself!
Sit with your drawing for a bit. Write about how you
feel looking at your vision board of affirmations.

Final Thoughts: Your Journey Awaits

Final Journal Prompt

It's your time to create the life you want on paper. Look back on all the writing you did for each lesson in this guide, and make it clear exactly what you desire and what you are calling in for yourself. Don't leave anything out!

After doing this exercise, condense it to a bullet list you can place on your bathroom mirror. Your job is to look at the list every day. You'll be surprised how your subconscious will help you achieve the life you want.

Beautiful soul, you hold the pen to your life's story. Remember, you don't need bangs to change your life—you need a life coach to guide you toward a life you've always dreamed of. Embrace every twist, take risks, and savor the journey as you become the fierce, empowered woman you were born to be. Your journey awaits, and I'm here cheering you on every step of the way.

With all my love,

Jody

Jody and Devin

Interested in being coached by me?
Send coaching inquiries to msjodyodell@gmail.com
or visit my website at msjodyodell.com.

....

....

....

....

....

....

....

....

....

....

....

....

....

....

....

....

....

....

....

....

Made in the USA
Columbia, SC
24 May 2024